"I" is for Indy
The World's Greatest Race

An A-Z Book for "500" Fans Who are Young and Young at Heart

Words by Mike King
Illustrations by John Rodgers
Foreword by Donald Davidson

To Nathan —
See you at Indy!
Mike King
voice of the "500"

Foreword
Donald Davidson, IMS Historian

The first time I encountered Mike King was quite a number of years ago when he was the public address announcer at the Terre Haute Action Track. I knew nothing about him yet, but I listened to his work during the event and thought he was quite outstanding. Because I have always been big on compliments, I climbed the stairs to the announcers booth to tell him that, never *dreaming* he would end up being the chief announcer for the Indianapolis Motor Speedway Radio Network.

When he first told me of his plans for this book, my initial reaction was that he might be facing quite a challenge in trying to produce something that would appeal to both youngsters *and* adults. How would it be possible, I wondered, for him to be able to write a paragraph or two describing a certain "500" tradition or rule, and still be able yo get the point across to *youngsters*, when some of these items aren't that easy to explain to *adults*?

And then there was the matter of illustrating the book in such a fashion as to appeal to enthusiasts of all ages.

What I did not know, until Mike showed me the first galleys, was that the illustrator he had chosen was John Rodgers.

What a master stroke!

John is a most interesting person and, from where I sit, a bit of a mystery. Not only does he *not* do this for a living, but he seems to have done a pretty good job of flying under the proverbial radar. "Quiet" and "unobtrusive" are understatements. I first became aware of him quite a while back when several people around the Garage Area started showing me amazing little paintings he'd done on, of all things, bottle caps! One day, I was approached by the man himself, and into the palm of my hand he placed a cap on which there was a tiny portrait of me! I was amazed.

As anyone who has ever attempted such a thing will know, drawing or painting a face that actually *looks* like the person it is intended to be can be HARD. And that's just on a *normal* surface, let alone a bottle cap.

Here, in Mike King's book, John has had the opportunity to spread out a bit and the results are remarkable, Not being an expert on art—other than for knowing what appeals to me, and what doesn't—I wouldn't know quite how to describe his style except to say that it is distinctively unique, captivating, full of life and obviously the gift of a God given talent. I could envision him building quite a following in the future as some sort of icon of pop culture. Case in point: When Mike showed two-time "500" winner Arie Luyendyk the piece of artwork that ended up being chosen for the cover, Arie's wife exclaimed excitedly, "Can I get a big version of that to hang on our wall?"

I understand, in the meantime, that John has also been doing this sort of thing for country and western artists, not on bottle caps but rather on *guitar picks*, and that he started to gather some attention in that field of endeavor.

So, racing enthusiasts young and old, sit down with this book and prepare to be thoroughly entertained. Hopefully, you will be reading interesting little nuggets from "Uncle Mike" you may not have known about before, and perhaps the mystery of some more complicated race procedures may finally be solved. And maybe John Rodgers will end up with a gig as an illustrator for *Mad Magazine*. Which is *intended* to be a compliment.

As far as Mike's personal choice for what each letter stands for, several of us suggested to him, right at the offset, that he would likely be forever fielding opinions from readers concerning what he *should* have gone with.

Well, you know what? I'd say that sort of leaves the door open for "Uncle Mike" to produce Volumes Two and Three.

"A" is for A.J.

Not one man, but two

Both built cars, one drove 'em
Both legends, that's true!

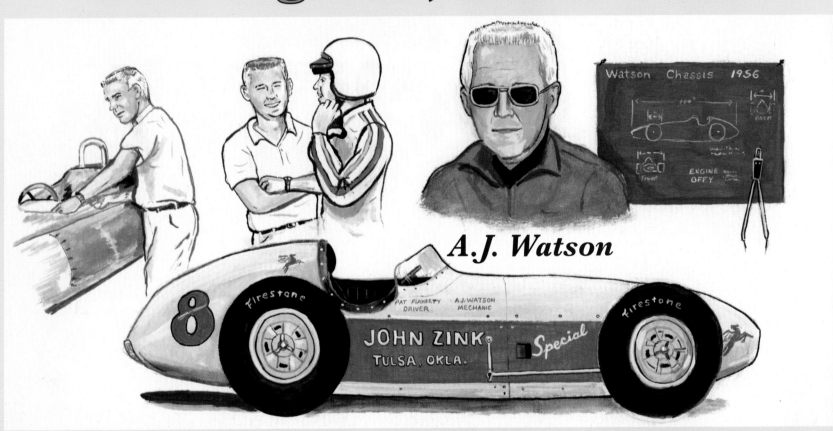

A.J. Watson

A. J. Watson is perhaps the most successful car designer and builder in the history of the Indy 500. His famed "Watson Roadsters" won at Indianapolis in 1956, 1959, 1960, 1962, 1963 and 1964 and are considered by many to be the most beautiful race cars to ever turn laps on the famed 2.5-mile oval.

The Legend of A.J. Foyt, Jr. was born at the Indianapolis Motor Speedway in 1961, when the tough Texan won his first "500" in a car design that was inspired by A.J. Watson. Foyt won again in 1964 driving a "true" Watson Roadster. An accomplished mechanic with a keen sense for engineering, Foyt helped design the Coyote chassis he won with at Indy in 1977. Regarded by many as the greatest race car driver of the 20th century, Foyt was the first driver to win the Indianapolis 500-Mile Race four times (1961, 1964, 1967, 1977). He added a fifth victory at Indy in 1999 as a car owner, with Sweden's Kenny Brack at the wheel.

A.J. Foyt

"B" is for Borg-Warner

The biggest and the best
If your face is on it, you were faster than the rest!

Weighing in at more than 90 pounds and standing more than 5 feet tall, the Borg-Warner Trophy was first awarded to Louis Meyer, the winner of the 1936 Indianapolis 500-Mile Race. The Borg-Warner Automotive Company commissioned designer Robert J. Hill and Gorham, Inc. to create what has become the most coveted trophy in motorsports.

Made of sterling silver, the Borg-Warner Trophy now bears the likenesses of all Indy 500 winning drivers along with a 24-karat gold likeness of the late Anton "Tony" Hulman (see "H").

and "B" is for Brickyard
A nickname, a fact...

In the early years bricks covered the track

The original surface of the Indianapolis Motor Speedway was crushed stone and tar, but for reasons of safety the owners decided to pave the track with more than 3 million bricks in the fall of 1909, earning the Speedway its nickname... "The Brickyard."

"C" is for Carnegie and Carburetion Day

"And Heeee's On it!"

Both are key ingredients during each month of May

Tom Carnegie will forever be an institution at the Indianapolis Motor Speedway. In 2005 he celebrated his 60th year as the Public Address Voice of the World's Greatest Race Course, and you can see a bronze plaque honoring Tom affixed to the Tower Terrace Grandstand Wall facing Victory Lane. Carnegie has many celebrated phrases.

Among them...

"And heee's on it"

(which Tom usually says when a driver begins a qualifying run)

and...

"It's a new track record"

* * * * * * * * * * * * * *

Carburetion Day is the final day that cars are allowed on the track before the start of the Indy 500. Generally referred to as "Carb Day," the schedule includes the final IndyCar Series practice session, and the annual pit stop competition.

By the way, carburetors haven't been used on cars that race in the "500" for quite some time, but the name lives on.

"D" is for Danica
Indy's First Lady of Speed
The fans jump and shout when her car takes the lead

Danica Patrick burst onto the scene at Indianapolis in 2005, driving for the Rahal-Letterman Racing team.

She wasn't the first woman to race in the 500, but Danica did make history as a rookie. Starting 4th (the best starting position ever for a woman at Indy) Danica fought her way back after falling to 16th, and on lap 191 passed Dan Wheldon to take over the lead.

Wheldon would regain the lead 3 laps later and would go on to win the 89th Indy 500, while Danica finished 4th.

Danica Patrick became the first female driver to lead the Indy 500, and the first female driver to complete all 200 laps; her 4th-place finish was the best ever by a woman at Indy, and she also posted the fastest lap of the month in 2005...229.228 mph!

Danica Patrick was the fourth woman to race at Indy. Janet Guthrie was first in 1977, followed by Lyn St. James and Sarah Fisher.

"E" is for Eddie Rickenbacker...the Ace

* * * * * * * * * * * * *

One of the early owners of this historic place

* * * * * * * * * * * * *

Capt. Eddie Rickenbacker became a national hero during World War I as a fighter pilot, but interestingly enough he had driven in the Indianapolis 500-Mile Race five times before he ever learned how to fly.

Rickenbacker headed up a group of businessmen that purchased the Indianapolis Motor Speedway in 1927 from its original owners, Carl Fisher, James Allison, Frank Wheeler and Arthur Newby.

It was Rickenbacker who was responsible for the
installation of a golf course on Speedway grounds
(now known as Brickyard Crossing).
Eddie Rickenbacker sold the
Indianapolis Motor Speedway to Terre Haute,
Indiana, businessman Anton "Tony" Hulman in 1945.

"F" is for Flagman

Keep your eye on his stand

The cars speed up and slow down with the wave of his hand

The flagman has always been a key figure in racing, and that's still true today. He's the guy who lets the drivers know what to do. His flags tell drivers when it's time to speed up, slow down, move over...and, in some cases, stop. He communicates with drivers by waving a special set of flags, each with a specific meaning.

Green means go, as fast as you can.
Yellow means slow down.
Red means stop.
The blue flag with the yellow stripe means move over, a faster car is coming up to lap you.
Black means your car has a problem or you broke a rule, so you have to go to the pits.
The white flag means one lap to go, and the checkered flag is waved at the end of the race.

The flagman for the Indy 500 used to stand on the track, but now has a specially designed stand above the famous "Yard of Bricks" (See "Y").

"G" is for Gasoline Alley and those four famous words...

"Gentlemen, Start Your Engines" It's the last command heard

The world's best drivers and their cars use Gasoline Alley
to make their way from the Garage Area at Indy to pit lane.
Cars that race in the Indy 500 haven't used gasoline since 1964,
but the name of that famous stretch has remained the same.

The command "Gentlemen, start your engines"
was made famous at Indy by 3-time 500 winner Wilbur Shaw
and still brings the crowd to its feet every race day.
The last command given to drivers before the start of the race,
it has been spoken by a member of the Hulman-George Family
every year since 1955, when Tony Hulman (see "H") stepped to the
microphone to start the event. With the addition of female racers
to the field the command has, at times,
changed to "Lady and Gentlemen, start your engines...."
and "Ladies and Gentlemen, start your engines,"
which was used in 2000 when both Lyn St. James and Sarah Fisher
qualified for the "500."

"H" is for Hulman... and Hulman-George, too

The family that rescued the "500" for fans like me and you

When Terre Haute, Indiana, businessman Anton "Tony" Hulman purchased the Indianapolis Motor Speedway in 1945, he saved both the track and the race from extinction.

The Speedway sat idle for four years during WWII, and at the time of the purchase the track was overgrown with weeds and most grandstands and buildings were in need of massive repairs.

Tony Hulman realized his dream of restoring the Indy 500 to its place of national and international prominence the following May, and since that race in 1946 the Hulman family has continued to own and develop the "World's Greatest Race Course."

Mari Hulman George, the daughter of Tony Hulman, chairs the Board of the Indianapolis Motor Speedway, while her son, Anton "Tony" Hulman George, is the President and CEO of the Indianapolis Motor Speedway Corporation.

Tony Hulman George

Mari Hulman George

"I" is for Indy
The World's Greatest Race
Since 1911 it's been setting the pace

A quartet of Indiana businessmen, Carl Fisher, James Allison, Frank Wheeler and Arthur Newby, financed and built the Indianapolis Motor Speedway in the spring of 1909. With the automobile industry growing by leaps and bounds, the facility was designed to be a year-round testing grounds for Indiana-based car manufacturers.

The original surface was crushed stone and tar, but for reasons of safety the owners decided to pave the track with more than 3 million bricks in the fall of 1909, earning the Speedway its nickname... "The Brickyard."

On May 30, 1911, the first Indianapolis 500-Mile Race took place, and after 6 hours and 42 minutes of racing Pennsylvania's Ray Harroun became the first winner of what has become known as "The World's Greatest Race." Now, nearly 100 years later, race teams and drivers return to Indy every month of May to chase the most prestigious title in racing..."Indy 500 Champion."

Drivers still race on the same track layout that was originally designed in 1909... a 2.5-mile oval configuration with four corners banked at just over 9 degrees. The front and back straightaways each measure 5/8 of a mile in length. Each turn is 1/4 of a mile long, and the two short straightaways or "chutes" connecting turn 1 to turn 2, and turn 3 to turn 4, each measure 1/8 of a mile.

Two hundred laps around the track make up the total 500-mile race distance. As speeds increased, the need for a smoother racing surface meant that most of the original bricks were paved over by 1961. The only bricks that remain can now be found at the start/finish line. Appropriately enough, that strip of bricks measures a yard in width (see "Y").

"J" is for Jim
Mr. Nabors...what a treat

The song that he sings brings the fans to their feet

Jim Nabors is the actor who gave life to the TV character "Gomer Pyle" in the 1960s on two legendary television programs... "The Andy Griffith Show" and "Gomer Pyle, USMC."

Still recognized around the world for his portrayal of that iconic character, Jim Nabors has also been a traditional part of the Indy 500 pre-race ceremonies for better than three decades. In addition to his skills as a great comedic actor, Jim Nabors is a great singer and his rendition of "Back Home Again in Indiana," which comes just minutes before the start of the race, is regarded by many fans as one of their favorite "500" traditions.

The song made its first appearance during the pre-race ceremonies at Indy in 1946 and was sung by James Melton of the New York Metropolitan Opera Company. Mel Tormé, Vic Damone, Ed Ames, Peter Marshall, Dennis Morgan and Dinah Shore are among the many other celebrities who have shared their rendition of the song. Jim first sang "Back Home Again in Indiana" in 1972, and in 2005 he made his 26th appearance in the Indy 500 pre-race ceremonies. In addition to earning a place in the heart of "500" fans, Jim also earned a star on the Hollywood "Walk of Fame" in 1991. When Jim Nabors isn't at Indy, or performing around the world, you can find him at his home in Honolulu, Hawaii.

"K" is for Kansas
It's some kind of state

Kansas has produced more multiple "500" winners than any other state to date!

It's true. Three natives of Kansas have won the Indy 500, and all three have won the world's biggest race more than once. Rodger Ward (born in Beloit, Kansas) won at Indy in 1959 and again in 1962. Johnny Rutherford (born in Coffeyville, Kansas) won the "500" in 1974, 1976 and again in 1980. And Rick Mears (born in Wichita, Kansas) won four times at Indy, 1979, 1984, 1988 and 1991. (See "M" for more on Rick Mears).

"L" is for Laps
It takes 200, you know
Unless the rain falls and shortens the show

From the drop of the green flag,
until the checkered flag waves,
drivers will race 500 miles at Indy
the last Sunday in May.
That means you have to travel
the complete distance around the track
(2.5 miles or 1 lap) 200 times in order
to complete the entire race.
There have been times when weather has prevented
the race from going the full 500 miles,
but thankfully, that's the exception
rather than the rule.

In the event that weather becomes a factor,
101 laps must be completed to make the race "official."
Should rain start falling one lap past the midway point,
race officials can decide to end the race early, giving
the win to the driver leading at that point.

"M" is for Mears
One tough driver to beat

Rapid Rick would strap in and then turn up the heat

1979
1984
1988
1991

Sat on
The Pole
6-Times

Rick Mears is one of the most popular and most successful drivers ever to race at Indy. Between 1979 and 1991 Rick won the Indy 500 four times, the pole position (see "Q") six times, set the single-lap track record five times and set the 4-lap qualifying record four times. In 15 career starts at Indy, Rick Mears recorded seven top-3 finishes. Interestingly enough, all 15 of Rick's starts at Indy came driving for the same car owner...Roger Penske (see "R"). Though a native of Kansas (see "K"), Mears grew up in Bakersfield, California. Rick's brother, Roger, also competed at Indy in 1982 and again in 1983.

"M" is also for Milk
It's the drink winners choose
but a swig of cold milk tastes good, even if you lose

The tradition of the Indy 500 winner drinking milk in Victory Lane goes back to 1936. Not wanting water, winner Louis Meyer told someone that a cold drink of buttermilk would sure "hit the spot." A couple of minutes later a bottle of buttermilk appeared, much to Meyer's delight. The American Dairy Association of Indiana now has a representative on hand in Victory Lane following each 500-Mile-Race with a selection of milk products. White, skim, low fat, even soy milk are available to the winner. And just in case there's another Louis Meyer out there, I'm sure they will gladly make buttermilk available.

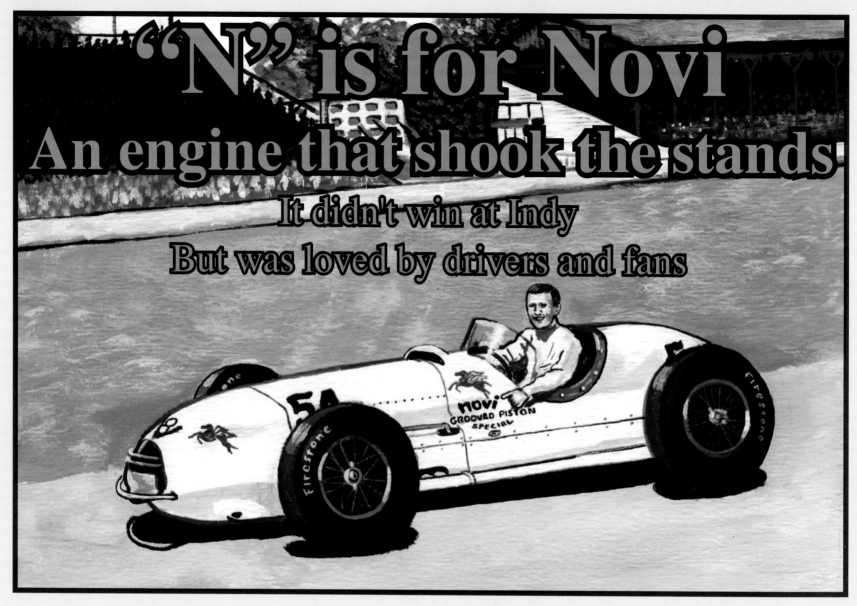

"N" is for Novi
An engine that shook the stands
It didn't win at Indy
But was loved by drivers and fans

Some of the world's greatest engine builders and car manufacturers have brought their powerplants to Indy, all hoping to win the "500." They include Maserati, Miller, Offenhauser, Ford, Cosworth, Duesenberg, Stutz, Ilmor, Porsche, Chevrolet, Mercedes-Benz, Ferrari, Peugot, Alfa Romeo, Cummins, Oldsmobile, Chrysler, Toyota and Honda. Some never won the "500," while several have enjoyed incredible success. Yet when you ask veteran Indy fans to name their favorite engine, one name is mentioned over and over. Novi.

The Novi engine made its first appearance at Indy in 1941, only then it was known as a "Winfield" because it was designed and built by the Winfield brothers (Bud and Ed) of California. There was no racing at Indy in 1942, '43, '44 or '45 because of World War II, but in 1946 the "500" returned...and so did the Winfield brothers. Only now their engine was known as a "Novi." The reason? Michigan businessman Lew Welch invested thousands of dollars to help develop the Winfield design. Welch decided to name the engine after the place in Michigan where many of his businesses were located: Novi, Michigan.

The powerful V-8 produced nearly 800 horsepower and powered the fastest car in qualifying on six different occasions...but the Novi never finished first in the race. Its best finish was 3rd in 1948 with Duke Nalon at the wheel. Those who heard it rumble around Indy during the month of May say the Novi's sound was unmistakable.

"O" is for Open Wheel
You'll find no fenders on these cars

Precision driving is the trademark
of Indy's greatest stars

The Indianapolis 500 has always featured "Open Wheel" race cars, which means that the wheels on the cars are not covered. As the cars got sleeker and faster, drivers and fans alike began referring to them as "Indy Cars." Racing an "Open Wheel" car requires an incredible degree of precision and concentration from the driver, because even light contact with another car can result in a crash. "Open Wheel" race cars that take part in the Indy 500 are among the world's fastest race cars (see "S"), turning laps during the race at better than 220 miles per hour!

"P" is for Pagoda and scoring Pylon, too

One helps fans keep track of the leaders, the other is a place with a great view

Two of the unmistakable landmarks at the Indianapolis Motor Speedway are the scoring pylon and the Pagoda. Both are located on the front straight, and both have undergone changes since first appearing at the track.

The original "Pagoda," named because its design was inspired by Japanese architecture, was built in 1913. It was replaced in 1926 with a new structure, which was used through the 1956 race.

Between 1957 and 1998 there was no Pagoda at the Indianapolis Motor Speedway. The building that overlooked the front straight at Indy was known as the Master Control Tower. A new ultra-modern Pagoda was erected in 1999.

The Pagoda offers some of the best views of the World's Greatest Race Course and houses race officials responsible for timing and scoring the event, race control, the IMS Radio Network (see "R"), several organizations that oversee fan safety and two suites for fans to watch all of the action.

The first scoring pylon was built in 1959 and stood 84 feet tall. The four-sided pylon displayed the positions of all 33 cars on the track at the same time. The original Scoring Pylon was replaced in 1994. Measuring 96 feet from the ground to the strobe light that flashes atop the pylon's flagpole, it can display the positions of all 33 cars while also giving the lap count and average speed of the race.

"Q" is for Qualifications
It's unique at this track
Four laps (that's 10 miles) and there's no looking back

The qualifying procedure for the Indy 500 is unique, to say the least. You can attempt to qualify during two weekends in the month of May. The first day of qualifications is called "Pole Day" because it's the only day you can win a front-row starting position. The inside spot on row one goes to the fastest driver on day one of qualifications. That spot is referred to as the "pole position," a term borrowed from horse racing, in which poles were used to support the fence on the inside of the track.

A qualification run at Indy requires speed and nerves of steel. Unlike most races, which allow you to take your fastest of two laps, a driver must complete four consecutive laps on the 2.5-mile course and take his/her 4-lap average for a qualifying speed. Traditionally, the starting field for the Indianapolis 500 is made up of the 33 fastest qualifiers starting in 11 rows of three cars each.

"R" is for Radio Network
and Roger Penske, "The Captain"

One has an incredible Indy record, the other describes all of the action

The Indianapolis Motor Speedway Radio Network has been providing live coverage of the Indy 500 to race fans around the world since 1952, making it the world's oldest continually operated motorsports network.

Because of the size and shape of the race course, and the worldwide importance of the event, 13 announcers are stationed at positions around the track, in the Pagoda, on pit lane and in the garage area in order to capture all of the action.

Team owner Roger Penske has established a winning record at Indy that will likely never be equaled. Penske first came to the Indianapolis Motor Speedway with his race team in 1969, and in the 36 years that followed Team Penske has celebrated in Victory Lane (see "V") as Indy 500 winners an amazing 13 times!

The Team Penske Indy winning driver roster reads like a "Who's Who" of Open Wheel racing (see "O").

That roster includes Mark Donohue (1972), Rick Mears (1979, 1984, 1988, 1991), Bobby Unser (1981), Danny Sullivan (1985), Al Unser, Sr. (1987), Emerson Fittipaldi (1993), Al Unser, Jr. (1994), Helio Castroneves (2001, 2002) and Gil de Ferrran (2003).

Why is Roger called "The Captain"? Because he runs the tightest ship in racing!

"S" is for *Speed*

Indy's such a fast track

Push that right foot to the floor or you'll wind up in back!

When Ray Harroun won the first Indy 500 in 1911 he averaged 74.602 miles per hour.

Seventy-nine years later (1990), Arie Luyendyk won the fastest Indy 500 in history, averaging 185.981 miles per hour.

Luyendyk, a native of Holland, returned to Indy in 1996 and established another record that will likely never be broken.

The "Flying Dutchman" set the speed record for qualifications (See "Q") with a 4-lap average of 236.986 miles per hour.

Included in that run was a lap clocked at an incredible 237.498 miles per hour!

"T" is for Tires

Important, yes they are, and Firestone has won more times at Indy by far

Since 1911 tire manufacturers have used the Indy 500
as a proving ground for developing new tire technology.
Companies like Goodyear, BF Goodrich, Michelin, Dunlop,
Palmer, Braender and even Sears have brought their tires to
Indy to compete during the month of May.
None of them have performed like Firestone.
Nine decades ago Harvey Firestone decided that racing
was the best way to showcase his tires, and heading into
the 90th running of the Indianapolis 500 his Firestone tires
have rolled into Victory Lane (see "V") at Indy 56 times.
Like the race cars, tires have changed drastically
since that first 500-mile race at Indy in 1911.
Because of the incredible speeds at Indy, only special
racing "slicks" are used. A "slick" tire has no tread pattern,
but instead offers a wide patch of rubber that helps to keep
the car glued to the track as it travels through the corners at
high speeds (see "S").
Because there is no tread on these specially designed tires,
cars never run in the rain during the month of May.

"U" is for Unser
This family's one of a kind

The "Als" and Uncle Bobby have won Indy 9 times!

The Unser Family has a long legacy in the Indianapolis 500 that dates back to 1958, the first year Jerry Unser started in the race.

Brothers Al and Bobby arrived a few years later... Bobby in 1963 and Al in 1965.

Al Unser, Sr. (Big Al), won the Indy 500 in 1970, 1971, 1978 and 1987. He's one of just three drivers to win the "500" four times. A.J. Foyt and Rick Mears are the other two members of that exclusive club.

Bobby Unser won at Indy in 1968, 1975 and 1981.

Al Unser, Jr. (Little Al), added two victories, taking the checkered flag in 1992 and 1994. Little Al's win in 1992 over Scott Goodyear remains the closest finish in Indy 500 history.   Only .043 of a second separated the 2 cars at the finish.

Robby Unser (son of Bobby) and Johnny Unser (son of Jerry) have also raced at Indianapolis during the month of May.

"V" is for Victory Lane
Such a popular place

If you get to park there you've won the Big Race!

The most popular piece of property on the grounds of the Indianapolis Motor Speedway is Victory Lane, but over the years that location has changed quite a few times!

When Ray Harroun won the first Indianapolis 500 in 1911 he wasn't sure where to stop, so he pulled off of the track and drove behind the Judges Stand that was located where the Pagoda now stands. A couple of years later Victory Lane was moved to the south end of the pit lane, toward turn one, and remained in that location through the 1970 race. In 1971 Victory Lane moved to the foot of the Master Control Tower (see "P") in an area called the "Horseshoe" because of its shape. Victory Lane made a short move in 1986 to a hydraulic lift located in front of the Master Control Tower and situated on pit lane. With the completion of the new Pagoda in 1999, Victory Lane made the move to its current location, adjacent to the "Victory Podium" at the base of the Pagoda (see "P").

"W" is for the Winners
So what's in a name?

A win that comes at Indy
brings you lifelong fame

WINNERS of THE INDIANAPOLIS 500

1911	Ray Harroun	1942	World War II - No Race	1975	Bobby Unser
1912	Joe Dawson	1943	World War II - No Race	1976	Johnny Rutherford
1913	Jules Goux	1944	World War II - No Race	1977	A.J. Foyt
1914	Rene Thomas	1945	World War II - No Race	1978	Al Unser
1915	Ralph DePalma	1946	George Robson	1979	Rick Mears
1916	Dario Resta	1947	Mauri Rose	1980	Johnny Rutherford
1917	World War I - No Race	1948	Mauri Rose	1981	Bobby Unser
1918	World War I - No Race	1949	Bill Holland	1982	Gordon Johncock
1919	Howard Wilcox	1950	Johnnie Parsons	1983	Tom Sneva
1920	Gaston Chevrolet	1951	Lee Wallard	1984	Rick Mears
1921	Tommy Milton	1952	Troy Ruttman	1985	Danny Sullivan
1922	Jimmy Murphy	1953	Bill Vukovich	1986	Bobby Rahal
1923	Tommy Milton	1954	Bill Vukovich	1987	Al Unser
1924	L.L. Corum	1955	Bob Sweikert	1988	Rick Mears
	Joe Boyer*	1956	Pat Flaherty	1989	Emerson Fittipaldi
1925	Pete DePaolo	1957	Sam Hanks	1990	Arie Luyendyk
1926	Frank Lockhart	1958	Jimmy Bryan	1991	Rick Mears
1927	George Souders	1959	Rodger Ward	1992	Al Unser, Jr.
1928	Louis Meyer	1960	Jim Rathmann	1993	Emerson Fittipaldi
1929	Ray Keech	1961	A.J. Foyt	1994	Al Unser, Jr.
1930	Billy Arnold	1962	Rodger Ward	1995	Jacques Villeneuve
1931	Louis Schneider	1963	Parnelli Jones	1996	Buddy Lazier
1932	Fred Frame	1964	A.J. Foyt	1997	Arie Luyendyk
1933	Louis Meyer	1965	Jimmy Clark	1998	Eddie Cheever
1934	Bill Cummings	1966	Graham Hill	1999	Kenny Brack
1935	Kelly Petillo	1967	A.J. Foyt	2000	Juan Pablo Montoya
1936	Louis Meyer	1968	Bobby Unser	2001	Helio Castroneves
1937	Wilbur Shaw	1969	Mario Andretti	2002	Helio Castroneves
1938	Floyd Roberts	1970	Al Unser	2003	Gil de Ferran
1939	Wilbur Shaw	1971	Al Unser	2004	Buddy Rice
1940	Wilbur Shaw	1972	Mark Donohue	2005	Dan Wheldon
1941	Floyd Davis	1973	Gordon Johncock		
	Mauri Rose*	1974	Johnny Rutherford		

* Boyer finished for Corum, Rose finished for Davis.

"X" Marks the Spot
Where you'll find the World's Greatest Race
Speedway, Indiana
What a great name for a great race place!

The builders of the Indianapolis Motor Speedway (see "I") chose a large tract of farmland located about 5 miles west of the city of Indianapolis as the site to construct the track in 1909. With the exception of a few farmhouses the land west of Indiana's capitol city was largely undeveloped, but it was connected to Indianapolis by railroad.

As the Indy 500 began to grow, so did the community surrounding the track. By 1914 the area began to become known as "Speedway City." In 1926 the word "City" was dropped from the name, and the Town of Speedway was incorporated. Speedway, Indiana, has its own town council, fire department, police department, school system, utilities and public library, along with approximately 13,000 residents who call the town home.

"Y" is for the Yard of Bricks
at the famed start-finish line

Cross them first, then kiss them...
you'll be remembered for all time

While the Indianapolis Motor Speedway was once paved with more than 3 million bricks (see "B"), now only a few hundred remain. You'll find them at the most renowned start/ finish line in the world. The strip of bricks that cross the track measures 36 inches wide—a yard of bricks—and they were among the original Culver paving blocks used to pave the track in 1909. In recent years, race winners at Indy have shown their gratitude by kneeling and planting a kiss on the yards of bricks.

"Z" is for Zenith
That means greatness, the best

* * * * * * * * * * * * * * * *

The "500" will always be
a notch above the rest

* * * * * * * * * * * * * *

It's the biggest, it's an icon, The Greatest Spectacle in Racing...
Until you've seen it you've missed out...it truly is breathtaking

Every May they come to Indy...racing fans from near and far
They anxiously await the start, to see those Indy Cars

The drivers come from far and wide to show the world their style
To be the fastest, to beat the best, to lead mile after mile

It's milk, it's Taps, a balloon release, a spectacle of color
It's 500 miles at Indy...The Race that's like no other!

About the Author

Mike King is the Chief Announcer for the Indianapolis Motor Speedway Radio Network, and begins his 8th year as the "Radio Voice" of the Indy 500 and the IndyCar Series in 2006.

A native of Winston-Salem, NC, Mike has called Terre Haute, Indiana "home" since 1986 and lives there with his wife, Nicole, who also happens to be a huge fan of racing, and their three great children...Tyler, Madison and Abigail. Like illustrator John Rodgers, Mike is a longtime racing fan who continues to be awed by the spectacle that is the Indianapolis 500 Mile Race. The name of the King family dog was even influenced by "The World's Greatest Race." The golden retriever-chow mix has answered to the name "Emmo" for 15 years. "Emmo" is the nickname of 2-time Indy 500 winner Emerson Fittipaldi.

Have a suggestion for Volume Two of "I is for Indy"? Contact Mike at: mking@brickyard.com.

About the Illustrator

John Rodgers has been blessed with a special talent, and he has been impressing family and friends with his artistic abilities since the age of 5. A native of Knightstown, Indiana, John is a lifelong fan of auto racing and has created works of art for many of the biggest names in the sport.

A multi-talented artist, John is also a sculptor who has created dozens of one-of-a-kind bobbleheads and figurines. His work is proudly displayed in trophy cases of 2-time Indy 500 winner Helio Castroneves and 2004 IndyCar Series Champion Tony Kanaan, in the office of Indianapolis Motor Speedway Corporation President Tony George and in the home of Nelson Stewart, father of 2-time NASCAR Champion Tony Stewart.

John and his wife, Kim, live in Brazil, Indiana. They are the proud parents of Andrea and Brad, and proud grandparents of Bryce and Chloe.

Learn more about John Rodgers and see more of his incredible work at: www.johnrodgersoriginals.com.

"I" is for Indy
Text © 2006 by Mike King
Illustrations © 2006 by John Rodgers

This book is available in quantity at special discounts for educational groups and organizations
For more information contact:
Witness Productions, Box 34, Church St., Marshall, IN. 47859. 765-597-2487.
or order online at www.lisforindy.com.

ISBN 1-891390-21-X

OFFICIALLY LICENSED

PRODUCT